POSTMODERN ENCOUNTERS

Baudrillard and the Millennium

Christopher Horrocks

ICON BOOKS UK

TOTEM BOOKS USA

Published in the UK in 1999
by Icon Books Ltd., Grange Road,
Duxford, Cambridge CB2 4QF
email: info@iconbooks.co.uk
www.iconbooks.co.uk

Published in the USA in 1999
by Totem Books
Inquiries to: PO Box 223,
Canal Street Station,
New York, NY 10013

Distributed in the UK, Europe,
Canada, South Africa and Asia
by the Penguin Group:
Penguin Books Ltd.,
27 Wrights Lane,
London W8 5TZ

In the United States,
distributed to the trade by
National Book Network Inc.,
4720 Boston Way, Lanham,
Maryland 20706

Published in Australia in 1999
by Allen & Unwin Pty. Ltd.,
PO Box 8500, 9 Atchison Street,
St. Leonards, NSW 2065

Library of Congress Catalog
Card Number: 99-071123

Reprinted 2000

Text copyright © 1999 Christopher Horrocks

The author has asserted his moral rights.

Series editor: Richard Appignanesi

ISBN 1 84046 091 1

Typesetting by Wayzgoose

Printed and bound in the UK by
Cox & Wyman Ltd., Reading

Introduction: Escaping the Millennium

In 1996, Jean Baudrillard was asked where he would be on the eve of the Year 2000. 'Anywhere out of this world!', he replied.[1] He had pithily summarised his position on the millennial 'catastrophe' by sardonically referring to a prose poem by Charles Baudelaire. Baudelaire, a 19th-century participant-observer of the alienation, 'inner heroism' and cultural contradictions of urban life, had given expression to his own anguished soul and its desire to escape, yet draw sustenance from, the confusion that characterised the emerging modern, urban world.[2]

This book describes the millennial thought of another French 'fugitive': Jean Baudrillard. Baudrillard, despite critics who accuse him of promoting style at the cost of substance, cannot be so easily aligned with his own cultural precursor. It should not be assumed that he enjoys the benefit of Baudelaire's historical 'window' in which to frame social, economic and cultural transformations in terms of their impact on a social critic's rarefied or neurotically attuned consciousness and experience. That was a feature of modernity that had, by the latter half of the 20th century, become more an encumbrance than a critical perspective. As we approach the end of the century, such intensities are simply those of the talk show.

Given our current era's complexity, Baudrillard is faced with the more daunting task of providing an analysis of a globalised culture in which all claims of the *unbearable* yet *revelatory* impact of the modern world on subjectivity have been rescinded. In, and after, the postmodern era, criticism no longer invests in the heightened aesthetic sensitivities that characterised the early critics and visionaries of industrial and technological change. For Baudrillard, there is no moment of self-realisation, either in the face of the banality of the world or in its poetic alternative.

The following discussion of Jean Baudrillard's encounter with the millennium explains and discusses his dedicated texts on the subject, both in the context of his project to date, and in the light of recent and relevant thought by philosophers and theorists in the modern period. The critique of his position is secondary, and is briefly discussed prior to Baudrillard's tantalising conclusion to the debate, by which time the radical character of his thought should be apparent, as will be the chasm that separates Baudrillard's ironic challenge to the world from Baudelaire's impassioned escape.

Background

Prophesying catastrophe is incredibly banal. The more original move is to assume that it has already occurred.[3]

Jean Baudrillard has published several texts on the Year 2000 and the millennium. His first explicit thought appeared as 'Pataphysics of the Year 2000', an essay published in France in 1992, which develops and synthesises conventional versions of the millennium as the end of history. The term 'pataphysics' refers to Alfred Jarry's 'science of imaginary solutions',[4] which challenged conventional science and reason itself (see 'Key Ideas' at the end of this book). To understand this term, we must recognise that the debate supersedes the common assumption that Baudrillard speaks only of 'simulation' in his essays, while acknowledging that his 1980s work on this subject is a key feature of his current position.

What is simulation? Simulation describes the late-modern revolution in communications, cybernetics and systems theory that generates sign systems organised not simply to *conceal* reality, but to *produce* reality from the models or codes of the mass media, the political process, genetics and digital technology. This model of reality by simulation from models is one which has historically succeeded earlier 'orders of simulacra' employing other forms of semblance: the Renaissance 'copy' which guaranteed the truth of the original; industrialisation's 'series', in which mass-produced objects referred not to an original or referent, but generated meanings in relation to each other. With the advent of communications systems, cybernetics and late capital's drive to mobilise itself through images and meanings rather than simple products, designated 'reality' is now no longer even absent but generated by models and codes in a self-referential manner, as *hyperreality*: reality now is more real than real.

As we move towards the millennium, a fourth order of simulacrum appears. This one has the character of the fractal, and is of a viral, exponential or 'metastatic' order. This order describes the tendency of systems or models that have supplanted reality to extend endlessly in dimensions intrinsic to their logic, yet with unpredictable and often chaotic outcomes. Baudrillard employs the metaphors of fractal science to suggest that culture too is infinitely divisible, proliferates cancerously, leads randomly and exponentially from the particular to the general, and from stability to instability. These fluctuations can lead to effects that are completely the reverse of the system's intentions, and subject to new organising principles that Baudrillard, employing chaos theory, calls 'strange attractors'. This is quite beyond rationalist claims to verifiability, truth and reality. It is obvious, therefore, that those thinkers still attached to a model of reality that stakes a claim in reason and judgement are upset with such a version of events. It is in this context that we must approach Baudrillard's millennial thought.

Beyond Linear History

The whole problem of speaking about the end (particularly the end of history) is that you have to speak of what lies beyond the end and also, at the same time, of the impossibility of ending.[5]

Baudrillard's views on the millennium cannot be separated from his hypotheses on history. He argues that history has disappeared with regard to modern linear time, since the latter can be considered as 'a purely artificial process'.[6] In fact, history as we understand it is a simulation, for it presents itself as a model of time that relies on the concept of an end, yet holds it always in suspense. For Baudrillard, history can only take place in this kind of simulated time, if we understand history as a succession of *non-meaningless* facts, each giving rise to the next by cause and effect, but doing so without any absolute necessity or plan. 'Everyone remains aware of the arbitrariness, the artificial character of time and history', Baudrillard claims.[7] And if our linear, progressive time is in doubt, then logically so too is the idea of the 'end', or the constant delay of the end. This end must be just as artificial. The 'illusion of the end' is a more likely explanation.

Baudrillard emphasises the point by contrasting our version of linear time with cultures where the 'end' is placed elsewhere, usually at the beginning of time. Unlike Judaeo-Christian modernity, there are other traditions that have a fulfilled order of time, and that no longer have to wait for the 'freedom' or 'arrival' that comes with the end. Certain belief systems outside or before ours have 'placed the crime at the origin once and for all'[8] and, rather than waiting for judgement in the future, tell stories of the perfection from which they originally sprang. Rather wishfully, Baudrillard says we should also put our end, and thus any remorse, behind us. This not being the case, there is at least a challenge to the end that has persisted during the millennium: the urge to anticipate, falsify and precipitate it through messianic beliefs, mass suicide or violent resolution. This millennial hurry must be seen, though, as rooted in the *secular* modern time of our current era's acceleration of events and processes, and attendant economic, cultural, political and even sexual 'exchanges'.

In his first essay on the millennium, Baudrillard quotes Elias Canetti, who claimed that, 'as of a certain point, history was no longer real. Without noticing it, all mankind suddenly left reality'.[9]

Canetti wrote this in 1945, when the atomic bomb had destroyed the last 'valid myth': the sun. With Hiroshima and Nagasaki, 'light is dethroned, the atomic bomb has become the measure of all things. The tiniest thing has won: a paradox of power'.[10]

Despite his horror of a world that had witnessed the A-bomb, the Holocaust and other events that made pre-war history seem Palaeolithic by comparison, Canetti nonetheless maintained that history could be recovered. However, Baudrillard, for different reasons, points to three hypotheses that discount this. Here, he presents the question of history as a linear process irrevocably disrupted by technologies such as communications and cybernetics.

Baudrillard's first idea is that modernity has accelerated to a point at which we have been ejected from a position in space and time where we were able to reflect our events back to ourselves with any endurance, and therefore consequence. This is because modern media have 'atomised every event', sending meanings, messages and images in every direction politically, historically and factually. Any theory or explanation can only 'tear concepts from their critical zone of reference',[11] wiping out time by sending events into a vacuum at the periphery in order to process them digitally and circulate them in computers, circuits and networks.

The second version reverses this thesis: history has slowed down, like light near a dense astral body. Baudrillard relates it to social theory and the 'silent majorities' of the mass population. Such is the density of 'cities, commodities, messages and circuits',[12] when they are absorbed into an indifferent social mass, that history cannot reach a speed necessary for it to transcend this inertia. History, Baudrillard concludes, will not be able to catch up with its historical end, caught as it is by the gravitational mass of social indifference. This analogy brings society into the equation.

The third analogy is termed the 'stereophonic effect' and refers to technologies that reach, for example, the perfection of digitally reproduced music. This simulation of music makes music disappear into its special effects of ultra-fidelity. Such a process, for Baudrillard, also figures in microphysics and in all cases where the gap between the event and its replay, or the cause and the effect, closes to the point where the latter, in its purity of reproduction (of music, of an event, of an experiment) casts doubt on the existence of the cause, such as pre-digital music. Unfortunately for Canetti, Baudrillard concludes, we can neither go back to real events or pre-stereo music, nor at a broader level find grounds to distinguish between true or false history, given their technical perfection. What key issues does this tripartite analogy raise?

First, Baudrillard has problematised the definition of time. What he calls 'real time' calls attention both to the cultural artifice of Western, linear, deferred history and to the immediacy and artificial directness of historical events as they appear in, for example, the news. Our obsession with reality suppresses the sense that events are happening elsewhere, and anticipates their end by freeing us from linear time in order to possess them in a postmodern 'now', almost before they have taken place. This demonstrates for Baudrillard our lack of confidence in the meaning or purpose of the event.

Second, Baudrillard identifies forms of cultural behaviour that occur as a consequence of the urge to apprehend reality, primarily in relation to the themes of memory understood as information storage, processing and retrieval. This amounts to Baudrillard's claim that history will replay itself through our technologies.

Third, it is apparent that Baudrillard's view of history is not one that sits tidily in 'endist' philosophy. History is not at an end. Rather, the idea of the end of history is itself an illusion. As Baudrillard has shown, this illusory end may have different forms, depending on the rhetorical figures that one uses to describe it.

His summary at the conclusion of 'Pataphysics' is that our generation has less and less confidence in history and digs in behind futuristic technologies and information stores. We are asleep but do not know it. The Year 2000 might not happen, but we will not know that.

Before we discuss the implications of Baudrillard's position, we should place his claims in the context of general thought on the 'ends' of history, particularly those pertinent to the postmodern and millennial period. This will bring us to a firmer understanding of his statement, in 1992, that the Year 2000 would not perhaps take place and that it is, in effect, behind us.

The Ends of History?

. . . in our age the myth of progress appears to have been largely exhausted. It has been replaced by the myth of modernity itself. The future has become almost as unreal and empty as the past.[13]

Matei Calinescu, cited above, clarifies the link between the crisis in modernity and the condition of decadence, where consciousness of the end of the world makes every instance decisive. Decadence is one consequence of restlessness, self-examination, agonising commitments, momentous renunciations and, above all, 'increased time awareness'. Yet can the end of progress go unchallenged? Is its key feature entropy and exhaustion, with decadence as a cultural compensation and nihilism a philosophical accompaniment?

These questions relate to Baudrillard's thought. It should be noted that Baudrillard's view of history stands outside the framework offered by many theorists of history, as it neither promotes its winding-down (the decadent and decaying version), nor its rejuvenation by philosophical or theoretical attempts to negotiate the *impasse* of Enlightenment and modern thought.

The discourse on 'endism' is one which, very broadly, consists of opposing views held by two groups. There are those who either mourn or deny the death of Enlightenment values, and so attempt to maintain their foundations against the perceived irresponsibility and abnegations of postmodernists, including Baudrillard. Others are instead counter-Enlightenment, and support a radical rethinking of value and the claims of history. In short, there is a theoretical and philosophical struggle over the end of history, and therefore the meaning of the millennium.

The ends of history have a complicated genealogy in Western culture. We can identify this genealogy starting from Kant, through Hegel, to Marx's effect on thought in the 20th century. As a necessary element of Enlightenment reason, history was philosophically conceived as inseparable from the realisation of an ideal of human freedom.[14] History was initially descriptive of the separation of reason from faith. This permitted rationalist inquiry into the relative subjective freedom of the individual to make cognitive, moral and aesthetic judgements in the world, according to secure criteria of truth, validity and social purpose.

Hegel's dialectic assumed that history's meaning lay in the arrival of freedom after an Idealist, quasi-religious pursuit of rational morality, and a struggle for universal and reciprocal 'recognition' of one's humanity, rather than a self-interested project. Hegel never imagined the struggle to preserve this freedom would end. Wars would continue after the end of this history, even though the American and French revolutions had satisfied a societal struggle for universal recognition of freedom.

Marx later defined history as progress in material terms. Only when society had collectivised social, economic and political life could freedom begin. However, in the late 20th century, history seemed not to be following the plot designed by such dialectical materialism. A rash of publications, such as Herbert Marcuse's *One-Dimensional Man* and Daniel Bell's *The End of Ideology*,[15] argued that the end of history had been short-circuited because the contradictions between classes in capitalism had been hidden by what amounted to instant gratification. The working classes, formerly conceived as the potential inheritors of the future, settled for welfare and consumer goods rather than responsibility. The ensuing debate asked whether this was a disaster or a happy outcome. Either it was a form of 'false consciousness' (society as unwitting dupe of mass consumption) – an ideological mask of 'real' economic conditions; or perhaps, as Francis Fukuyama controversially argued in the 1980s, it might be one aspect of a liberal democratisation of the world that effectively spelt the end of totalitarian regimes as a viable historical possibility. While such states have not achieved democratic stability, Fukuyama says, 'liberal democracy remains the only coherent political aspiration that spans different regions and cultures around the globe'.[16]

Baudrillard refuses to countenance so dialectical an end to history. 'This is not the end of history in Fukuyama's sense', Baudrillard replies, 'by the resolution of all the contradictions to which it had given rise, but the dilution of history as event: its media *mise en scène*, its excess of visibility'.[17] Everything has become available as history, or 'historicalised', and so the term has lost its transcendental value. America, for example, has become a utopia without illusion, and one of excess, banality and levelled-down equivalence. This should demonstrate, *contra* Fukuyama, not a completion of history but its definitive non-accomplishment.[18]

What characterises the versions of history outlined above is an investment in Enlightenment, modern and progressive definitions of history: namely, the values of reason, truth and critique. Habermas is a recent variant of the philosopher who sees modernity as an 'unfinished project', in which 'communicative action' would strive towards Enlightenment values of public speech free of distortion and injustice.[19]

However, there is a counter-Enlightenment strand to the question of the end or completion of history, which can be traced with qualification from Nietzsche to Baudrillard.[20]

Friedrich Nietzsche, in his *Unfashionable Observations* of 1874,[21] criticised historical inquiry in his time for making the present look like just another episode, and the creative acts of individuals humble by comparison. It burdened individuals with more knowledge than they could absorb; it encouraged a resigned relativism because change implied that the present was unimportant; and it generated irony and cynicism because it engendered a sense of late arrival. In *Human, All Too Human*,[22] Nietzsche argued for a new 'historical philosophy' to replace metaphysical philosophy, which, he argued, was only a poor substitute for religious belief.

For late 20th-century followers of Nietzsche,

there are radical postmodern lessons to learn. Lyotard, for example, considers Nietzsche's 'will to power' as the primacy of the imagination in inventing criteria in the absence of rules. We must invent criteria.[23] Nietzsche claims that the modern scientific world view is an extension of the Christian one based on faith in truth, which encourages an ascetic attitude: the repression of desire. This faith in truth is closely linked to Baudrillard's attack on the metaphysical and objective aspects of scientific, rationalist and technological constructions of reality.

Baudrillard has taken stock of Nietzsche's famous argument:

What then is truth? A moveable host of metaphors . . . which, after long usage, seem to a people to be fixed, canonical, and binding. Truths are illusions which we have forgotten are illusions . . . [24]

Truth for Nietzsche is ambiguous at best, and at worst is placed in the service of decay and death. 'Self-conscious illusion' is the vital alternative. The place of 'illusion' and truth in Nietzsche's work is of great importance to the form of Baudrillard's argument. The latter says that Nietzsche wrote magnificently of the 'vital illusion':[25] the perspective on the world, history and truth in which one takes truth for fiction. If, on the other hand, we un-selfconsciously treat illusion objectively as a reality and, as Calinescu notes, endow it with the 'moral' prestige of truth, 'we blind ourselves to its nature and become the slaves of a lifeless dogma'.[26]

Baudrillard must go further than Nietzsche to set up illusion as a form immanent in the late-postmodern world's phenomena and events, produced within a technologically integrated reality of mass communications and digital rationality. In our era, therefore, the relation between truth and fiction is far more complex. Nevertheless, Baudrillard shares with Nietzsche the realisation that modernity cannot be escaped, but only radicalised from within.

Baudrillard's image of history as an acceleration in modern technology is rendered more urgent in his reference to the 'decadent' philosopher E. M. Cioran. Cioran wrote that our machines were not driving humanity to its doom, but were invented for man 'because he was already on his way there; he sought means, auxiliaries to attain it faster and more effectively'.[27] For Cioran, there is no goal to progress, and modern society is no more conscious than earlier civilisations: 'each period is perfect in itself – and perishable.'[28] Baudrillard, however, does not see technology as merely symptomatic of a human death drive. Causes and effects, characterised as human agency and inhuman outcomes, are much more reversible in Baudrillard's millennial equation, as are decadence and reflections on the end of the century from the point of view of other cultures. He claims that decadence is narcissistic, as 'the idea of the decadence of the West is part of its cultural language. The West has always delighted in imagining its own death. I don't seek to locate the counterpoint to the West'.[29]

Whereas Cioran saw democracy as weak and flabby for having expelled violence as a negative value, and the Balkans as strong for preserving it, Baudrillard states that democracy sets up new forms of anomalous violence in terms of enforced interactivity and participation, and a freedom that leads to anomalies *inside* the system. Baudrillard therefore neither sets up a dialectic between East and West, nor adopts a nihilistic position. To point out the short-circuiting of history is not to believe in 'nothing', but simply to 'register this curving back of history and try to thwart its lethal effects'.[30] This effect is one of registering and accounting for history after it has passed, without the comfort of nihilism or annihilation. History is not intent on ending as such. Indeed, for Baudrillard, history is now being sent into reverse.

Repenting and Recycling: the 20th Century Reactivated

The fact is that, in a sort of enthusiastic work of mourning, we are in the process of retracting all the significant events of this century, of whitewashing it, as if everything that had taken place . . . were merely a hopeless imbroglio, and everyone had set about undoing that history with the same enthusiasm that had gone into making it.[31]

Nietzsche asserted that the measure of human life was the test of eternal recurrence: we should live our life as if we had to do so again and again. Baudrillard's version is driven instead by the 'back-handed' immortality of a retroactive and interminable history.

Baudrillard's thesis on history tends to switch between themes without announcing the fact. We can, however, identify key points in his retroactive versions of history.

First, Baudrillard claims that history consists of a revival of previous or repressed values and energies, such as freedom in the Eastern Bloc. Second, the motive for such revivals is to reactivate values in order to launder, purify or 'positivise' history as repentance for the present. Third, these revived values do not appear in their original form, but are only circulated as extreme versions without their historical significance. Fourth, such accelerated recycling and revival of old conflicts and values effectively means that history itself is running backwards, so that these recycled forms can make no historical sense whatever. Fifth, there are certain values that cannot readily be recycled. These are similar to waste-products or residues. One task of the millennium is to dispose of these.

The millennium is defined above all by humanity's desire to find absolution in the past. We do this, Baudrillard contends, by reviving the best and worst of modern history in order to distinguish what was good from what was evil. He describes this as millennial 'hysteresis', which defines for him the continual growth of history, politics, the social and ideological, even after they have lost significance. Not only is there an exploration into 'what went wrong' in the modern era, but the emergence of millennial processes of 'restoration, regression, rehabilitation, revival of the old frontiers, of the old differences, of particularities, of religions – and

even resipiscence in the sphere of morals'.[32]
Humanity's errors are recognised everywhere, and
altered in order to neutralise them in a topsy-turvy
rewriting and rehabilitation of the 20th-century
energies – to undo the 20th century enthusiastically
by *re-doing* it.

*Thus, when we speak of the 'end of history', the
'end of the political', the 'end of the social', the 'end
of ideologies', none of this is true. The worst of it all
is precisely that there will be no end to anything,
and all these things will continue to unfold slowly,
tediously, recurrently, in that hysteresis of everything which, like nails and hair, continues to grow
after death.*[33]

For Baudrillard, the millennium is analogous to the
weakened body in which illnesses, once dormant,
are reactivated. Cancer, for example, reprises the
unbounded reduplication of cells in the embryo in
excess of its objectives and as a useless revivalism.
The analogy may seem strained, yet it does fore-
ground the late 20th century's 'retro' scenarios.
These are not only those of media, culture and
fashion, but include, for example, regional conflicts
reactivated after the Cold War. History at the

millennium, Baudrillard says, is rifling through its own dustbins and looking for *redemption* in the rubbish by dusting off and re-circulating old ideologies, values and regimes. From postmodern art, which reappropriates recent or current culture, to the collapse of the Berlin Wall, it seems that we are consigned to an infinite replay of all that happened before.

However, the desire to restore certain energies by recycling them and putting them back into history is not to be confused with their original state. The thawed Eastern Bloc freedom, for example, released in its dramatic, active, violent, transcendent form as an Idea, would only destabilise the West's millennial version of freedom as a consensual and virtual psychodrama. Recycled values have to join a speeded-up remake of history, and one that knows no distinctions. Recycled historical freedom after the Berlin Wall's collapse includes Chernobyl, Russian gangsterism and imported pornography, as well as defrosted human rights.

Baudrillard humorously shows this mismatch between reactivated values and their relation to history by using the cryogenic example of Walt Disney. Frozen in liquid nitrogen, he dreams of being revived in a better, more advanced world. But he may in fact regain consciousness in the 18th century, the Ancient Egyptian world, or any other scene he once staged in Disneyland as a fantasy or projection. The irony that awaits Walt Disney is one we are attempting to contrive.[34]

Yet is this condition one of nostalgia or mourning – a realisation that things have come to an end and might somehow return? Baudrillard refutes this, and argues that we are left with melancholia and resentment at the disappearance of the dream of the end and the origin. Any attempt to get into reverse in order to avoid the empty simulations that now confront us fails. The harder we try to rescue the real or the referent, such as the 'meaning' of war, the more we fall back into such simulations as the Gulf War. Baudrillard introduces this 'reversing of the sign of catastrophe' in order to claim that there will be no future catastrophe, because the 'lost object is behind us', be it nuclear war or revolution.[35]

History, muses Baudrillard, has perhaps *always* been non-linear and open to strange reversals. As such, it is more like an anagram or palindrome than a sentence, and the playful confusion of history's rhymes and spoonerisms allows us to sense forms that are capable of providing a poetic alternative to the disenchanted confusion, the chaotic profusion of present events that attests to the suspension of the millennium's significance. This 'strike' of events epitomises the refusal of any occurrence to signify anything whatever, to have no import other than an *anticipated* meaning, constituted in its programming and broadcasting.

History today is too real and too immediate, as the events that should constitute it have no time to develop outside of the media. The narrowing down of history to 'current events' transforms history into the 'real time' of the news. The prodigious event, Baudrillard states, 'the event which is measured neither by its causes nor its consequences but creates its own stage and its own dramatic effect, no longer exists'.[36] This, for Baudrillard, is the true end of history, but not the finish, as history is now necrophagous and calls for new victims and events *to finish with them a little bit more*. It becomes clear for Baudrillard that history, as it functions near the millennium, can only be an exercise in recycling and waste-management.

When the present and future are deep-frozen, all excrement, Baudrillard conjectures, rises from the past. Failed ideologies, obsolescent utopias, outmoded concepts and fossilised ideas persist in our polluted mentality. 'Historical and intellectual refuse pose an even more serious problem than industrial waste. Who will rid us of the sedimentation of centuries of stupidity?'[37] The solution that millenarian culture has found is to recycle all this waste in order to offset history's fall from cyclical time.

Baudrillard's concept of the 'residue' that the millennium requires extends to the natural world, which for him has become an encumbrance that we cannot dispose of. Technological and industrial structures that condense functions, models and programmes make the habitat look like a surplus and a problem. We know, for example, that nature has become waste when it becomes recognised in law as having rights, as these are conferred by the law to give nature official recognition once it has disappeared. Humanity, with the rise of human rights, also becomes idealised and promoted in the image. Just as charity exists only with destitution, so too man's 'abjection' becomes essential to the perpetuation of 'rights'.[38]

Again, Baudrillard's observations do not add up to a description of a world in which events are simply the artificial products of the media, whose content was analysed as the 'manufacture of consent' by earlier critics such as Noam Chomsky, or characterised by Marshall McLuhan as a radical restructuring of the social by new communications systems.[39] Neither is Baudrillard trading in the *fait accompli* of the liberal democratic global order that Fukuyama suggests. In fact, Baudrillard's position points to much higher levels of instability in the relation of history, meaning and its reproduction. Things are not as settled as critics from left and right imagine. While we must examine the place of technology, media and globalism in Baudrillard's discussion of the millennium, we should be wary of accusing him of irresponsibly hastening the end by reducing reality, truth and history to a by-product of the role of media and other simulation models. This is far from the case, though his critics think otherwise. We turn now to the question of technology in Baudrillard's thought.

Technology, Simulation and the 'New'

The distinguishing traits of existence in late capitalist society, ranging from commercialization in the form of a totalized 'simulacrization' to the consequent collapse of the 'critique of ideology' . . . do not represent . . . dehumanization, but instead gesture toward a possible new human experience.

Gianni Vattimo

Gianni Vattimo, in his book *The End of Modernity*, employs Arnold Gehlen's term *post-histoire*[40] to argue that a positive opportunity resides in the crisis of the end of history and modernity. Reiterating Gehlen's point that modernity is in crisis because it has been 'secularised', he too concludes that progress today is just the routine production of consumer society that requires a constant and unchanging version of the 'new' to ensure the system's survival. However, this 'ever new' dissolves the meaning of progress as forward movement, thus producing the experience of the 'end of history'. The 'new' is, instead, what allows the world to stay the same. This profound immobility of technology is recognisable in works of science fiction (and in poor readings of Baudrillard, it should be said), where experiences of reality are reduced to the consumption of images, or the 'air-conditioned, muffled silence in which computers work'.[41]

The postmodern technoculture may represent the crisis of progress, truth and human values; but the philosopher Vattimo has attempted to wrest a positive version of thought from the collapse of our models of knowledge and being. Vattimo's position starts with a study of humanism's crisis from Heidegger's perspective. Heidegger judges the setting up of our technological world (the *Ge-Stell*) as the most advanced version and the logical outcome of Western metaphysics, in which the rational domination of a world of *objects* is rationalism taken to its objective completion. Humanism's defence of values such as freedom, truth or reason cannot, therefore, convince us that its values are an alternative to technological ones, since its own traits belong to those of metaphysics. Humanism is metaphysics.

The postmodern crisis is occurring not because technology threatens the values of humanism, but rather because technology has revealed the outcome to which these values must inevitably lead. Vattimo claims that to escape the domination of technology, and the rationalist objectivising thought that supports it, is to imagine with Heidegger that the essence of technology is not something technological. We must refute technology's own inescapable and unique reality, its cogency and necessity, and its laws must become subject to the same kind of philosophical scrutiny as the rationalist metaphysical thought from which it derives.

Vattimo coins the term 'weak thought', which refers to a form of consciousness that undermines the efforts of technological civilisation to impose its own version of the world as the sole possible reality.

This is a postmodern and philosophical version of thought that weakens technological reality's claims to effectiveness, while at the same time refusing to countenance nostalgia for the humanist claim that the human subject is at the centre, controlling and ordering the world of objects. Vattimo's 'weak thought' believes neither in metaphysical, technological nor humanistic reality. It attempts to experience science and technology as contaminated by other languages of contemporary culture, to show how the world of reality can be made 'lighter' by seeing that it is less sharply split between truth, on the one hand, and fiction, information and images on the other.[42] This is what, in the millennium, Vattimo calls an 'accomplished nihilism' that calls us 'to a fictionalized experience of reality which is also our only possibility of freedom'.[43]

While writers such as Charles Levin think that Baudrillard's approach is aligned with the '*laissez-faire* position of liberal postmodernists',[44] like that of Vattimo and Richard Rorty who see nihilism as our only chance, Baudrillard's reaction to Vattimo's will to fiction and resolution of metaphysical truths, human values and technological reality is clear: '*pensiero debole* [weak thought] *truly* is a feeble-minded form of thinking'.[45]

The difference in perspective lies in Vattimo's persistence in attributing the capacity to make the world a fiction to us as a capacity of thought, and therefore a philosophical enterprise. For Baudrillard, this surely must seem too subject-centred, and a gross underestimation of the vengeful and ironic effects of the world, fictional or not, that we try to represent or capture objectively. Worse, we can consider Vattimo's philosophy of technology as one that, by aligning technology with metaphysics and humanism as logical and rationalistic, completely fails to see the perversity, the reversibility and the chaotic kernel within the objective world of technology, including even weak thought as its pale reflection. Computers have viruses too!

Baudrillard confers on technology a more flexible role than either Vattimo or Heidegger. One of these roles is wit, exemplified for him by the cassette carrying information on AIDS that also carries a virus. Postmodern philosophers who attempt to call a truce between humanism and technology are unaware of other ruses more relevant to the late 20th century. Rather than being alienated by technology, or performing 'weak thought' on it, 'behind his doubles and his prosthesis, his biological clones and his virtual images, man takes advantage of these things to disappear'.[46] Answer-phones leave messages for us, and video recorders watch films in our absence. Computer crashes or slips of the hand on a computer mouse give the files we were compiling a value they should not have, when they are erased or inadvertently lost.

In such observations, we can see that Baudrillard's view of millennial technology neither defends the human from the machine or code, nor gives the victory to technology. Communications technology has a task to perform on our behalf. Through its vitiating processes, it takes on the role of exhausting our faith in reality. Similarly, the illusionism of mass communications and mass culture in all the confusion of ideologies, stereotypes, spectacles and banalities provides us with an intelligence test. For where better can we learn to question every image or commentary? Television breeds indifference, distance, scepticism and apathy. By making the world into an image, it numbs the imagination and produces adrenalin surges that simply lead to disillusionment.

'If you take one-thousandth of what you see on the TV news to heart, you're done for', Baudrillard says. 'But television protects us from this. Its immunizing, prophylactic use protects us from an unbearable responsibility.'[47] There is, however, a perfectionism to virtual technology that casts us in the role of an extinct species, or an inert residue more in keeping with traditional models of technological alienation. A compact disc, for example, does not wear out with use. This fact leads Baudrillard to suggest that it is as if the user had not used it, and therefore did not exist. Moreover, the virtual technology of the media's perpetual 'reality shows' is, Baudrillard suggests, related to the Dadaist 'ready-made'. He is referring to the artist Marcel Duchamp's famous urinal, extracted from the world to become a 'ready-made' work of art. Endless individuals are likewise removed from their everyday lives to act out the drama of their AIDS or marital problems on TV.[48] So it is we who become available as 'ready-made' slices of life for the code of media.

It can be argued that those postmodernists who promote fiction over reality fail to see that fictionalising the world is a job already assigned to technology, in which the 'perfect crime' of the world's realisation through the transformation of all acts and events into information and data is a form of extinction. Baudrillard refers to Arthur C. Clarke's story, 'The Nine Billion Names of God', in which

Tibetan monks bring in experts from IBM to compute all of God's names. Their task completed, and the prophecy of the end fulfilled, the technicians walk back down the valley as the stars wink out one by one. Our technologies, in other words, have worked out the end *ahead* of time.

Unlike Vattimo's idea that fiction could keep technological reality in check by revealing its metaphysical credentials, Baudrillard sees that technology absorbs the illusion of the world and its vision into *tele*reality, into 'real time' and into the virtual which – as Vattimo cannot see – is the opposite of illusion: total disillusion and disappearance. All those objects we 'critiqued' – such as history, power, work, dreams and sex – have exerted a revenge by vanishing, leaving criticism with no option but to do to the same. Weak thought is, in this context, like the last person at a party whose reason for remaining has therefore gone: 'Even more than the industrial machines, it is the machinery of thought itself that is laid off.'[49]

The result of this absorption of illusion by technological reality is that credibility – a property of objects and images – has taken the place of belief – a property of ourselves as subjects. We judge events by their proximity to their code or model, rather than by some metaphysical or humanistic principle. It is because of this that all discussions of millennial events are not so much a question of belief – of testing the subject against the object – but of credibility, verification and definition. Once God and truth cease to be radical illusions and simply objects of belief, belief becomes vulnerable to critique, which later collapses under the tests of credibility, or the 'convincingness' of the object or image. So it is that belief in the Gulf War is secondary to its credibility as a newsworthy and objectified event. Our only option is to question the manifest reality of the war by giving force to its illusory quality, rather than supporting or condemning it. Here, at least superficially, Baudrillard is aligned with Vattimo,[50] except that Baudrillard's will to fiction is more a challenge to the technological 'reality' of war, media and CNN than a 'light' and delicate path trod by philosophers in order to gain a positive human experience at the end of modernity.

The Shadow of the Millennium and the Final Countdown: Baudrillard's Final Thesis

In 1998, Baudrillard published two final essays on the millennium which prove to be his definitive analysis of the event. Many of the key themes of the previous discussions reappear. Moreover, the essays are a condensation of Baudrillard's work since the 1970s.

Baudrillard introduces his summary with an observation of a banal event. A digital clock on display at the Pompidou Centre in Paris displays the millions of seconds left until the Year 2000. This clock is the perfect symbol of the end of the century, as it counts *down* time. In this phenomenon, Baudrillard detects Western culture's particular crisis with history, because a countdown not only demonstrates that we confront our millennium as we would a bomb, but that we construe time as sub-traction and exhaustion rather than accumulation. For Baudrillard, history and time no longer grow from an origin in the past, but are being reduced to zero. It is Baudrillard's analysis of this process, and the culture that generates it, which concerns us here.

The clock at the Pompidou Centre, Baudrillard later discovered, was actually removed by the authorities before the countdown was completed. Was it because they wanted to ward off millennial effects, or were they scared it might unleash a real event at the dawn of 'Y2K', as global media corporation CNN depressingly calls it? This suspension of the event is also significant for Baudrillard. It tells him something about events in the millennial period and the Y2K event in particular. The non-event of this 'numerical fix', presumably ignored by many cultures, conceals the true important consequence of the end of the century – which is simply that the century has ended. The magic of the numerical event freezes other events of potential importance. Europe, the single currency, cloning and other events become suspended in the anticipated void – in the shadow – of the 'approaching asteroid' of Y2K. This stasis is similar to an electoral deadline (or a Presidential scandal) which freezes political life a year or more in advance. The vortex is filled with processes of recycling and repentance, not only in relation to our century's laundering of dirty money, corrupted consciences and the polluted planet (in order to arrive at a politically correct balance sheet), but also to ethnic and racial 'cleansing'.

We long, however, for any event that could arrive in the rarest of ways, unexpectedly and unpredictably from *another* history, and we require an answer to the question we have posed as the problem of the end: 'Are we at the end of history, beyond history, or still in an endless history?'[51] How do we jump over the shadow of the millennium,

Baudrillard asks, when the century's history is already finished and we are now constantly reliving it as an interminable crisis, with only an anorexic dimension that sees the finish as impossible?

Baudrillard raises the question of what lies beyond the end.

Well, beyond the end, there is virtual reality, that is to say, the horizon of a programmed reality in which all our physiological and social functions (memory, affect, intelligence, sexuality, work) gradually become useless.[52]

Our problem is one of dealing with events that do not take place, in a globalisation that is not progressive but splintered; in a world not of modern growth but outgrowth: *excroissance*. Baudrillard adds another dimension to his millennium that has flourished in his work since the 1980s: the acceleration of extreme phenomena that send previous modern historical processes into overdrive and so are, for example, no longer of the order of movement but of exponential power; no longer of change but passage 'through the limit', where ideas end in excess and history ends as information and instantaneous news events. As Terry Gilliam's film *Twelve*

Monkeys showed us, linear time is now reversible, so we 'recreate the world even before the emergence of the human race to see what it would be like without us or, even beyond humankind, to get a feel for what things could look like once we are all long gone; finally, to reinvent an origin, but only as a simulation, with definite limits'.[53]

Recreating everything is a 'therapeutic' obsession, and implies a 'not-here' of memory as a counterpart to information as the 'not-here' of the event. This feature appears in cultural fossilisation, in which art is made and then goes into museums before having had the chance to undergo the test of history. Obsessional neurosis, which attempts to forget the present by reduplicating the past, turns things into heritage before they pass through history. Spielberg's film *Jurassic Park* shows how instant DNA dinosaur-clones emerge too suddenly and destroy their fossilised ancestors' remains, before being exterminated too. Baudrillard says that *we* are also compressed between simulated origins and simulated ends: between fossils and clones. We are prey to what we thought was dead and past, which returns to strike at the heart of our sophisticated and vulnerable systems. With AIDS, even death's role as part of the countdown is emphasised.

It is at this stage in the argument that Baudrillard introduces his pataphysical explanation: the 'end of history' is simply one of history's many tricks. History has made us believe it has ended, when it is already *going in the other direction* by playing back wars, ethnic conflicts, nationalist and religious uprisings as part of history in the unmaking, and thereby changing their significance. After losing their historical vitality, events can now be re-broadcast on the transpolitical stage of the news media, thus creating truth in dubbing, post-synchronising and subtitling. However, it may be the case that *the world has duped technology*. Before discussing this radical conclusion, we should describe the millennial order to which it relates.

The Millennial World Order: Globalisation, Singularity and the Universal

Globalization is the globalization of technologies, the market, tourism, information. Universality is the universality of values, human rights, freedoms, culture, democracy. Globalization seems irreversible; the universal might be said, rather, to be on its way out.[54]

Baudrillard's fragmented and essayistic style often distracts readers from his rigorous and consistent perspective on the predicament of the millennial era. While his critics remain convinced that Baudrillard is an apologist for the status quo, or that he fails to deal with issues of inequality, injustice and oppression, or avoids active critique of institutions, ideologies or multicorporate capital, there is a sense in which Baudrillard is committed to challenging radically the assumptions that underpin the values and operations of culture and society and the solutions or readings offered by thinkers from the left and the right.

Baudrillard's scenario is straightforward. In the millennial era, there is a global system of exchange, a universality of values and a *singularity* of forms such as language, culture and individuals, as well as ones of chance and accident. Because universal values such as equality, democracy and human rights are losing some legitimacy and authority, they are less able to mediate and integrate singularities (individual, antagonistic forms and cultures). These universal values have been swept away by globalisation, so that all that remains is the 'all-powerful global technostructure standing over against the singularities which have gone back to the wild state and been thrown back on their own devices'.[55] Humanist intentions lead to unpredictable effects. 'High-definition democracy', Baudrillard jokingly contends, in which screens flash up humans rights charts like weather charts, will one day show violations of rights across the planet, but will actually worsen the situation.[56]

We can detect, therefore, a world that is not historically completed by history's universal values, but only integrated. However, globalisation is unstable and prone to violent, anomalous and irrational reversals from the perspective of 'enlightenment', and these may take ethnic, religious, linguistic, temperamental or neurotic forms.

This framework provides Baudrillard with the means to detect ironic reversals and unforeseen events that highlight the millennial game played between the global and the singular. Baudrillard's ability to keep pace with the effects of the global order places many other critics in a position where they have to resort to models of philosophical and political thought that look archaic, unwieldy and inappropriate for an era in which universal values are overstretched by globalisation and undone by singularities.

Baudrillard also highlights the reversibility of

universal values such as humanitarianism, democracy, freedom of speech and information, at a
global level in terms of their oppressive forms. For
example, the 'Sentimental Order' of the late 20th
century allows us smugly to condemn, launder and
expiate the West's exploitation of what was once
called the 'Third World'. In fact, what is more ger-
mane is the current moral and sentimental exploitation of that poverty as 'charity cannibalism'. We
exchange pity and compassion for the spectacle of
the destitution of others. This is a new energy
source, Baudrillard claims, and one that manages
the 'Fourth World' (the southern hemisphere's
beleaguered regions) as a residue in order to allow
the West to absolve and whitewash itself.[57]
International solidarity, humanitarian interference
and bloodsucking protection follow. Baudrillard
sardonically observes that because the initial problems were of the West's making, it is only fair that
we should profit by them. Indeed, we need catastrophes like a drug, and poor countries supply
them. In doing so, we defer the crisis and, with the
assistance of the media, live off catastrophic
cannibalism and perpetuate it in moral modes by
means of humanitarian aid. This production of global
reality is similar to the way in which economic

assistance maintains under-development. Both ensure the continuity of catastrophe.

In fact, regions like the Middle East, South East Asia, Africa and Latin America are overproducing disaster. Their floods, earthquakes, famines, ecological disasters and massacres are exchanged with our few paltry tornadoes, the manufactured catastrophes of economic crashes, car pile-ups, computer viruses and millennium bugs, as well as our future pre-programmed ones in genetics and cybernetics. Those regions therefore have a symbolic advantage, and we are envious of these biblical and glorious events. God ignores us. Additionally, with prices of raw materials crashing, the West will not pay adequately for the staple goods on which it lives. These other countries reply by exporting the only overpriced (illegal) commodity that can maintain their existence – drugs – and therefore pay off their world debt by exporting degeneracy and death at fantastic prices.

The outcome of a neutralisation of all forms outside of the globalisation of universals, is our own elimination. When illness, death, negativity, violence, strangeness, racial and linguistic differences are eliminated in the name of difference, we have annihilated singularity in order to radiate complete positivity. This, however, only ends in our destruction. Our millennial pursuit of hope is through signs of misfortune, just as global warming compels us to seek out coldness and austerity.[58]

Baudrillard's disdain for human rights depends on his argument that the unremitting positivity of such values hides a greater contempt for the world. Thus he accuses the lobbyists who promote respect for life (expressed in the view that no idea is worth someone's death) of trading on the insignificance of ideas and people in a scene without risks and sacrifices. Refusal to risk life is worse than its destruction, and is the fundamental nihilism. It is this nihilism that Baudrillard rejects.

If we add the West's compulsion to pity those who risk all, then Baudrillard's view of reality is clear. It is a problem for the West because we think reality has to be saved. The people of Sarajevo, for example, are forced into our panicked attempts to preserve reality through a hyperreal media and humanitarian harassment. Baudrillard complains that 'We have to go and retrieve a reality for ourselves where the bleeding is'.[59] However, the so-called 'victims' do not face this problem, as they do what they do without ends, or without compassion towards themselves. *Our claim that their reality ought not to exist is in fact a reality that exists just as it is.* That is what being 'real' means. As such, it is a rare experience.

A similar problem emerges with racism, which should have declined with the advance of democracy and the discrediting of racism's spurious genetic and theoretical justifications. Yet, the erosion of the singularity of cultures has actually led to a phobic relationship of the self to its artificial other, in the absence of genuine strangeness. It is the by-product of planet-wide conviviality and indifference.

Racism is desperately seeking the other in the form of an evil to be combated. The humanitarian sees the other just as desperately in the form of victims to aid . . . The scapegoat is no longer the person you hound, but the one whose lot you lament. But he is still a scapegoat. And it is still the same person.[60]

Baudrillard underlines the desperation of this situation, in which reasoned, logical and progressive solutions remain unthinkable. Behind all his diagnoses of globalised mentality, however, is the vulnerability of the system that finds itself globalised. The millennium is not simply the triumph of technological reason.

Extreme, Viral, Metastatic: Y2K as Proliferation

As politics, the social, the economic, the sexual and the aesthetic expand limitlessly, they become more transparent. The more they distend, the less they exist as themselves. This excessive millennial world is described by Baudrillard in terms that metaphorically describe the effects that our millennial forms have on a range of phenomena, from social identity to Internet viruses.

Baudrillard discusses our millennial era as one of obscenity and obesity, both of which exemplify our passage from modern growth to excrescence, 'from movement and change to stasis, ekstasis and metastasis'. These forms supply the end with excess, 'with hypertrophy, with proliferation, with chain reaction, with an overstepping of the mark. Not with lack, but with precisely the opposite'.[61]

We can see that this is far removed from Vattimo's sense that science and technology can be gently 'contaminated' by art and culture to show their arbitrary reality. Baudrillard's version is much more viral and extreme.

This process leads to a kind of total positivity, which puts an end to negation and exterminates through excess. Freedom is annihilated by liberation;

truth is extinguished by verification; community is liquidated by communication; forms are suffocated in information, and history is ended by the event. Much like cancer or a computer virus, millennial events are strange, random and chaotic, and not recognisable in terms of historical reason. Utopia now is no longer a problem of historically changing how life is lived (maximal utopia), but one of *survival* after the short-circuit of history: a minimal utopia. Even our technology senses this, as computers have 'equipped themselves with a number of functional gremlins, electronic viruses and other negative side-effects which protect them from perfection and spare them, in their turn, from pushing to their limits'.[62]

Our 'perfect crime' would have been to produce a fully integrated, flawless version of reality, and withdraw from it as historical subjects without leaving clues that we were once in history. Fortunately or not, we cannot do this, as germs, viruses and catastrophes act as signs of imperfection, and are our 'signature' in the simulated world. They ensure that we can imagine we exist.

Everywhere, anomalous events and individuals either exhibit themselves as 'extreme phenomena' that describe the system which extends beyond its own limits, or as fatal strategies – those antagonistic reversals that have turned back on a system's initial objectives. The former is characterised by any system that reaches excess (like information systems storing so much data that it would take years to collate), and the latter by the rebound, for example, of individual failure, disorder and delinquency as direct consequences of social programmes.

Within this scenario we should assess what still passes for the millennial human condition. What chances for the species in this catastrophic equation? And what possibility for humanity, now that it is simply a genetic code?

I.D. 2000: the Posthuman Condition

Before our era, Hegel, Marx, the Frankfurt School and the Situationists dreamt of the end of alienation, the liberation of the subject (ourselves) from an inauthentic and alienated relation to life, work and culture. Unfortunately, it may be that their dream of the liberated human subject came true to a horrifying degree. The humanist subject did not regain himself in his freedom once alienation ended, but merely became a fulfilled owner of an identity, rather than a subjectivity for which he would strive. All dreams of freedom have vanished.

Desire, the body and sex will all have been mere utopias like the rest: Progress, Enlightenment, Revolution, happiness. We are already avoiding the sun for fear of cancer (with an eye to the resurrection of bodies?), we have given up sex on account of the danger, we express ourselves less and less in public, we have stopped smoking, drinking, screwing. The New Political Ecology is on the march. Watch your personal equation! Keep your minds on the survival of the species and have as little fun as possible![63]

'Neo-individualism' describes social being after the age of bourgeois individualism, which once forged subjectivity through a battle between free will and alienation. The neo-individual is characterised by performance, athleticism and entrepreneurial hero-ism. Alienation is a luxury long gone, as it allowed the subject to imagine it could be other than what it was. Alienation has, however, now succumbed to 'identity logic': the millennial subject has become the *same as itself* and only related to others through *difference* rather than radical otherness. As Baudrillard claims: 'Identity is a dream pathetic in its absurdity. You dream of being yourself when you've nothing better to do. You dream of that when you've lost all singularity.'[64]

We can see this conversion in terms of the genetic revolution. Whereas humanism was once defined in terms of a person's virtue, gifts, essence, qualities and the innate freedom he had the right to exercise, it is now framed by human rights which above all wish to *preserve* the individual as an identity and as a species. However, Baudrillard argues, it is difficult to determine whether we have any rights over our 'selves' now that the technocracy has decided that we share nearly all our genomes with apes, and marginally less of them with mice. Again, however, ninety percent of the human genome is residual and seemingly superfluous to our existence. Should we claim this as ours by right?

Baudrillard's purpose in asking these questions is to show how humanism's idea of freedom and transcendence is wiped away in the genetic order of endless experimentation on our species. Myths of evolution, natural selection and death have been left behind in favour of the quest for artificial, 'domesticated' and technical immortality.[65] This is another form of disappearance in the face of the erasure of the inhuman and human boundary. This 'immortality', however, will contain no principle of antagonism or 'evil' because the viruses, germs, and threat which would supply it will be banished. In this sanitisation, the human species loses all immune systems, and faces itself without illusions or threat. This is a catastrophe.

It is clear that for Baudrillard the signs that were once particular to humanity are vanishing. The symbolic space and the vital illusions of dreams, utopias, ideal projects, death and the body are exterminated in their mobilisation by the 'new order'. Even desire becomes problematic, now that the radical otherness between male and female gives way to millennial cloning of sex with no purpose, where sexual functions will no longer be needed for reproduction. All that remains is a pure anatomical difference, meaning that real otherness collapses into conflicts over 'orientation' in the transsexual era. Sexual exchange now involves locking on to each other in new machinic rituals of switching, merging or commutation, rather than gazing seductively and fatally. Difference has replaced otherness, so that the only extremes we have left are excessive forms projected by and mirrored in the subject. Sexual identity, for example, has led to men hysterically caricaturing women in pornography. Women reply hysterically by turning the male into a case of sexual harassment. These are two sides of the same hysterical indifference.

The body has undergone not just radical and obvious changes in relation to technology and science, but also in relation to our mentality. The millennial body is treated in the same way that men treat women and women respond to men: as a fetishistic investment or cult. The body becomes exciting in its proximity or resemblance to a model of perfection, rather than in terms of an 'other' or transcendent ideal. The body is versed in the white magic of identity rather than the black magic of otherness:

This is how it is with body-building: you get into your body as you would into a suit of nerve and muscle. The body is not muscular, but muscled. It is the same with the brain and with social relations of exchanges: body-building, brainstorming, word-processing.[66]

Muscles are like 'character armour', and whereas women once wrapped their selves in their image, and in a narcissistic relation to an ideal self, body-building now effaces that comfort with the gymnastic Ego-ideal: stressed, toned, artificially self-referential and cold.

This, we can see, follows Baudrillard's analysis of

the demise of the 'other', leaving the poor subject-who-is-no-longer-one, because subjectivity would presume a struggle with otherness or alienation. All we have left are the monstrous variants of identity that develop artificial otherness while annihilating others. This is an autistic, isophrenic, fiercely tautological,[67] horizontal, scrambled madness, rather than the previous transcendent madness of schizophrenia and alienation. *The modern individual gives way to the millennial Selfsame.* After the modern hysteric[68] who acts out his terror at not being present to himself, comes the postmodern *allergic*, who reacts to the excessive presence of his 'being there'.

Millennial 'body-morality' ensures that we can dispense with Marx. Our expenditure of energy is no longer related to work but to leisure, to gym-time, where the virtually disabled[69] (all of us who use keyboards, drive cars or employ other prosthetics) can work off 'stress' in body-building, step-classes or other novel exercise regimes.

Baudrillard declares that we should neither become, nor be reconciled with, our body, our self, the other, nature – nor reconcile male and female or good and evil. The New International Hygienic Order can be seen everywhere jogging or walking, phobically concerned with bodies, self-maximisation and self-inflicted servitude.

Glory, destiny and conquest, and all the risks nature would have supplied us in this scenario, have become the challenge of the body against itself in ever finer grades of performativity and experimentation. This is why disabled Olympic athletes mutilate themselves to improve their chances, or cripples drag themselves to the top of Mount Kilimanjaro. The millennial neo-individual *invents* risks rather than faces them in destiny. The fight for survival disappears as he artificially recreates the conditions of survival.[70] There are no more heights – just dangerous sports.

The millennium, therefore, has not been designed for heroes and destinies. Rather, the dominant identity of the millennial neo-individual is that of the victim. The 'new victim order' organises otherness around the wretched, deprived, frustrated, handicapped subject, and the victim's strategy is to recognise himself in this 'necrological mirror' of guilty conscience.[71] Everyone is obsessed with gaining status as a victim in a new contract, as a response to their lack of conviction, as a response to the state's decree that they should take charge of their own lives, and as a consequence of being a species that is repenting and recycling catastrophe, a process in which all 20th-century gains in freedom are withdrawn, including sex, tobacco, alcohol, speeding and abortions. Liberated activities are now liquidated and seen as harmful to victims.[72]

Following this, now that everyone is liberated and told to look after themselves, they are faced with the realisation that they do not *want* to be free. There is a paradox in this, Baudrillard states, because 'the people liberated are never the ones you think: children, slaves, women or colonial peoples. It's always the others liberating themselves *from them* . . . Hence the dramatic concern of children to ensure that parents don't stop being parents, or at least that they do so as late as possible . . .'.[73] Baudrillard's solution, as with Sarajevo, is to fight without victimhood, starting out from evil, never from misfortune.[74]

The wretchedness and destitution of society is amplified by political and sociological discourses, in which sociologists replicate the deficits and misfortunes of their social object. Whereas culture, as the historian Michel Foucault said, was once obsessed with confessing sex,[75] it now confesses its wretchedness. Political correctness, as a millennial laundering, turns blacks into 'people of colour', the handicapped become 'differently abled' and prostitutes become 'sex workers'. This is a doctoring, Baudrillard concludes, that is 'more obscene than what it is trying to hide'.[76] In this setting, the singular destiny and sacrificial identity of AIDS sufferers is now only witnessed as an emotional contagion, giving rise to self-pity and self-disgust, which finds similar national expression in various mental Thanatons such as Live Aid, Comic Relief, Children Aid and World Aid – collective atonements for bad conscience and pornographic orchestrations of national unity.

Such is the condition of the millennial neo-individual and the non-destiny of the human species in Y2K.

Beyond the Millennium: Anti-Baudrillard, the Vital Illusion and the Return of the Mirror People

It is beside the point to condemn Jean Baudrillard for either spurning the tasks of rational and ethical judgement set by philosophers, or for his 'failure' to account for real human injustice, misery and oppression. Christopher Norris, Douglas Kellner, Alex Callinicos and a host of other writers in the Kantian or Marxist tradition have taken

Baudrillard to task, accusing his 'trash-theory' of being part of a modernist sensibility that substitutes art for philosophy, value for truth, image for reality, or Baudelaire for Kant.[77]

Yet people do support Baudrillard's right to comment on our condition. For example, sociologist Zygmunt Bauman has attacked those rationalist critics of Baudrillard who assume that criticism only carries weight if one's feet are set on the rock of absolute and universal truth. These critics are always the last to claim that their stance is part of historical, social and mundane transformations.[78] As Chris Rojek notes, Baudrillard's tone and style is hardly one of indifference or happy consumerism. Rather, Baudrillard writes like 'a man who is strapped to the mast of the pathological society, who sees everything without illusions and who accepts that there is no cure around the corner'.[79]

In fact, Baudrillard himself puts forward his critics' standard complaints. These apostles of reality and truth, he says, claim that he is monstrous for discrediting reality while there are so many in the world who find even existence difficult; that he fails to attack affluence on behalf of the poor; that he disparages class struggle when there are those who have not had their revolution; or that he insults feminism and human rights when many have not yet acquired those rights. Baudrillard sees, however, that these good intentions disguise a contempt. In phrasing reality as a version of life insurance or a human right and, worse, assuming that people place hope only in the visible proofs of their existence ('a plaster-saint realism'), such critics take them for naive and feeble-minded. This contempt simply reflects the desire of the propagandists of reality to reduce their own lives to an accumulation of facts, evidence, causes and effects. 'Well-ordered resentment always begins at home', Baudrillard concludes.[80]

After the Millennium: Baudrillard's Endgame

In the last passages of Baudrillard's article, 'The End of the Millennium or The Countdown', the enigma of the millennium is revealed, but any solution is held in suspense.

Jean Baudrillard's millennium can be seen as 'regulating and ordering the radical becoming, the radical illusion, of the world and its appearance', and 'reducing any internal singularity – of events, beings or things – to the common denominator of reality'.[81] However, we must also consider his millennium as a mirror in which every simulated object, every simulated identity, hides a defeated enemy that waits to burst out and shatter simulated reality.

So, everywhere, objects, children, the dead, images, women, everything which serves to provide a passive reflection in a world based on identity, is ready to go on to the counter-offensive. Already they resemble us less and less . . . I'll not be your mirror![82]

Thus Baudrillard sees a situation in which singularities emerge even when, and because, the system has become universal. These are joined by the extreme phenomena on *this* side of the mirror: the virulence of financial crashes, AIDS, computer viruses, deregulation and disinformation. Once discovered by science or anthropology, objects such as primitive societies, viruses or atoms are not content simply to remain themselves: they infiltrate the system. In this way, Baudrillard suggests, rationalist, scientific and technological subjects such as medicine, for example, must be pitied, as they are disarmed in advance by illnesses in which microbes are already interactive and capable of adapting to medication, in the way that insects adapt to insecticides.

At another level, Baudrillard sees a form of hope in the rise of 'world stupidity',[83] as it must surely lead to a violent reaction of some sort, unless such acceleration simply ushers in ever more banal acts. While our world's experts imagine solutions to achieve social provision, galloping exclusion ensues. In the same form, educational progress is outstripped by mental retardation.

One solution, Baudrillard suggests, lies in looking at worlds other than our own that have not undergone 'development' or, thankfully, that have failed at it. The future lies with such adolescent, confused societies that have not bought into the historical categories of humanism and reason.

In the concluding passages of 'The End of the Millennium', Baudrillard presents pataphysical aspects in which everything around us passes beyond its own limits and beyond the laws of physics and metaphysics. This stage, Baudrillard reiterates, is an ironic one. This propels us beyond even Heidegger's view of technology as the culmination of metaphysics, and allows us to consider science, media and technology ironically.

This ironic destiny is such because it reverses our assumption that technology controls, manipulates and alienates the masses. A more subtle approach to the millennium is to consider how the media, for example, is manipulated by the masses through their indifference to meaning, or how the social body allows political power to think it is in control, when in fact it is power that is vulnerable to destabilisation.

The essence of Baudrillard's argument is this. The subject, such as science, technology or political power, may imagine that it controls its object, such as nature, the masses and the world. Yet this scenario (which gives rise to models of oppression or alienation) may be reversible. *The object may be playing with the subject,* natural phenomena with science, the masses with the media, and so on. This is the objective irony of our era. Baudrillard gives an example . . .

Through the most subtle procedures we deploy to pin it down, isn't the scientific object toying with us, presenting itself as an object and mocking our objective pretension to analyse it? Scientists are not far from admitting such a thing today, and this irony of the object is the very form of a radical illu-soriness of the world, an illusoriness which is no longer physical (of the senses) or metaphysical (mental or philosophical), but pataphysical, to use the term Jarry applied to the 'science' of imaginary solutions.[84]

Ruse, irony, illusion, denial, reversibility, duplicity and radicality are not only conditions of our humanistic subjectivity, but conditions of the world. If we think beyond the conventional wisdom that the modern world of technologies, images and events signals alienation, expropriation, loss of will and history as a failed adventure, then we could detect a kind of 'showing-through' of the illusion of the world in the techniques we use to transform it. This is our millennial irony. Technology, in its apparent hyperreality, its high-definition and its supposed victory, might in fact be the ruse played on us by the object, in order to hide it and allow it to continue. Like Nietzsche's veil, technology hides the radical illusion and maintains the secret: the world playfully allows us to act out our dreams of control. This is the answer that lies at the 'end' of the millennium, but one we are not permitted to discover.

We must choose between the first and second hypothesis, between the 'perfect crime' of simulation's murder of reality and the objective irony of the world's disappearance behind technology – two irreconcilable yet 'true' perspectives. In Baudrillard's encounter with the millennium, these two versions of the world must be considered at once. 'There is nothing that allows us to decide between them.'[85] The millennium's catastrophe is perhaps our century's greatest trick.

Epilogue

When asked for his current thought on the millennium, Baudrillard replied, 'I have nothing new or original to add'. By becoming silent, Baudrillard has effectively withdrawn from the event a year in advance, reluctant perhaps to leave evidence of his involvement so close to the coming catastrophe. This has the makings of a perfect getaway.

Notes

1. The interview was published in *Icon Review*, Autumn 1996, p. 8. The text was incorrectly edited as '. . . somewhere in this world', showing that for one person at least, the idea of escaping the millennium was unthinkable.

2. '. . . It always seems to me that I should feel well in the place where I am not, and this question of removal is one which I discuss incessantly with my soul. . . . At last my soul explodes, and wisely cries out to me: "No matter where! No matter where! As long as it's out of this world!"' Charles Baudelaire, 'Anywhere Out of the World', *Twenty Prose Poems*, trans. Michael Hamburger, London: Jonathan Cape, 1968, pp. 56–7.

3. Jean Baudrillard, *Cool Memories II: 1987–1990*, trans. Chris Turner, Cambridge: Polity Press, 1996, p. 68.

4. 'Pataphysics' was created by Alfred Jarry (1873–1907). It concerns itself with the particular, rather than universal truths, and seeks to explain the laws governing singular exceptions by providing imaginary solutions. A typical example, employed by Baudrillard to describe how events and history are pulled away from their centre, runs as follows: 'Instead of formulating the law of the fall of a body toward a center, how far more apposite would be the law of the ascension of a vacuum toward a periphery.' See Roger Shattuck and Simon Watson Taylor (eds.), *Selected Works of Alfred Jarry*, New York: Grove Press, 1965; and Charles Levin, *Jean*

Baudrillard: A Study in Cultural Metaphysics, Hemel Hempstead: Prentice Hall Europe, 1996, pp. 277–8.

5. Jean Baudrillard, *The Illusion of the End*, Cambridge: Polity Press, 1994, p. 110.

6. Ibid., p. 7.

7. Ibid., p. 8.

8. Op. cit., Baudrillard, 1996, p. 69.

9. Op. cit., Baudrillard, 1994, p. 1. See also Elias Canetti, *The Human Province*, trans. Joachim Neugroschel, London: André Deutsch, 1985, p. 69.

10. Op. cit., Canetti, 1985, p. 67.

11. Op. cit., Baudrillard, 1994, p. 2.

12. Ibid., pp. 4–5. Baudrillard examines this phenomenon in *In the Shadow of the Silent Majorities*, New York: Semiotext(e), 1983.

13. Matei Calinescu, *Five Faces of Modernity: Modernity, Avant-Garde, Decadence, Kitsch, Postmodernism*, Durham, NC: Duke University Press, 1987, p. 247.

14. See Georg Wilhelm Friedrich Hegel, *Philosophy of Right*, trans. T.M. Knox, London: Oxford University Press, 1967.

15. See Herbert Marcuse, *One-Dimensional Man*, London: Ark, 1986; Daniel Bell, *The End of Ideology: On the Exhaustion of Political Ideas in the Fifties*, New York: Free Press, 1962.

16. Francis Fukuyama, *The End of History and the Last Man*, London: Hamish Hamilton, 1992, p. xiii.

17. Jean Baudrillard, *Paroxysm: Interviews with Philippe Petit*, trans. Chris Turner, London and New York: Verso, 1998, p. 8.

18. Ibid., p. 88.

19. See Jürgen Habermas, *The Philosophical Discourse of Modernity: twelve lectures*, trans. Frederick Lawrence, Cambridge: Polity Press, 1988.

20. Baudrillard, it should be noted, has always been suspicious of the term 'postmodern'; it describes the phenomena that he examines, rather than his own position.

21. See Friedrich Nietzsche, *Unfashionable Observations*, trans. Richard Gray, Stanford, CT: Stanford University Press, 1995.

22. See Friedrich Nietzsche, *Human, All Too Human*, trans. R.J. Hollingdale, Cambridge: Cambridge University Press, 1986.

23. Jean-François Lyotard and Jean-Loup Thébaud, *Just Gaming*, trans. Wlad Godzich, Minneapolis: University of Minnesota Press, 1985, p. 17.

24. Friedrich Nietzsche, 'On Truth and Lies in a Nonmoral Sense', in *Philosophy and Truth*, trans. and ed. Daniel Breazeale, Sussex: Harvester Press, 1979, p. 84.

25. Op. cit., Baudrillard, 1994, p. 94.

26. Op. cit., Calinescu, 1987, p. 186.

27. E.M. Cioran, *The Fall into Time*, 1964, quoted in Calinescu, 1987, p. 149.

28. E.M. Cioran, *A Short History of Decay*, trans. Richard Howard, Oxford: Basil Blackwell, 1975 (originally published 1949), p. 146.

29. Op. cit., Baudrillard, 1998, p. 41.

30. Ibid., p. 8.

31. Op. cit., Baudrillard, 1994, p. 32.

32. Ibid., p. 32.

33. Ibid., p. 116.

34. Jean Baudrillard, *Simulacra and Simulation*, trans. Sheila Faria Glaser, Ann Arbor: University of Michigan Press, 1994a, p. 13.

35. Op. cit., Baudrillard, 1994, p. 121.

36. Ibid., p. 21.

37. Ibid., p. 26.

38. Ibid., p. 79.

39. See Marshall McLuhan, *Understanding Media: The Extensions of Man*, London and New York: Ark, 1987; Noam Chomsky, *Manufacturing Consent: the political economy of the mass media*, New York: Pantheon Books, 1988.

40. Arnold Gehlen, 'Die Säkularisierung des Fortschritts' (1967), in *Einblicke*, vol. VII, ed. K.S. Rehberg, Frankfurt: Klostermann, 1978.

41. Gianni Vattimo, *The End of Modernity: Nihilism and Hermeneutics in Post-modern Culture*, trans. and intro. Jon R. Snyder, Cambridge: Polity Press, 1988, p. 7.

42. Gianni Vattimo, *La fine della modernità*, Milan:

Garzanti, 1985, p. 189. See op. cit., Vattimo, 1988, p. liii.

43. Op. cit., Vattimo, 1988, p. 29.

44. Charles Levin, *Jean Baudrillard: a study in cultural metaphysics,* Hemel Hempstead: Prentice Hall, 1996, p. 114.

45. Op. cit., Baudrillard, 1996, p. 36.

46. Jean Baudrillard, *The Perfect Crime*, trans. Chris Turner, London and New York: Verso, 1996a, p. 40.

47. Op. cit., Baudrillard, 1994, p. 63.

48. Op. cit., Baudrillard, 1996a, p. 28.

49. Op. cit., Baudrillard, 1996a, p. 27.

50. See Jean Baudrillard, *The Gulf War did not take place*, trans. Paul Patton, University of Sydney: Power Institute, 1995.

51. See Jean Baudrillard, *In the Shadow of the Millennium (Or the Suspense of the Year 2000)*, trans. François Debrix, 1998b (Internet publication), http://www.ctheory.com/a61.html, 26 September 1998. Originally Jean Baudrillard, *A l'Ombre du Millenaire ou le Suspens de l'An 2000*, Paris: Sens & Tonka, 1998.

52. Jean Baudrillard, 'The End of the Millennium or The Countdown', *Theory, Culture and Society*, London: Sage, No. 1, February 1998c, p. 2.

53. Op. cit., Baudrillard, 1998b.

54. Op. cit., Baudrillard, 1998, p. 11.

55. Ibid., p. 14.

56. Jean Baudrillard, *Fragments: Cool Memories III,*

1991-95, trans. Emily Agar, London and New York: Verso, 1997, p. 71.

57. Op. cit., Baudrillard, 1994, p. 66.

58. Op. cit., Baudrillard, 1996, p. 81.

59. Op. cit., Baudrillard, 1996a, p. 134.

60. Ibid., p. 132.

61. Op. cit., Baudrillard, 1998c, p. 5.

62. Op. cit., Baudrillard, 1996a, p. 40.

63. Op. cit., Baudrillard, 1996, p. 34.

64. Op. cit., Baudrillard, 1998, p. 49.

65. Op. cit., Baudrillard, 1994, pp. 89–100.

66. Op. cit., Baudrillard, 1996a, p. 125.

67. Op. cit., Baudrillard, 1996, p. 27.

68. Op. cit., Baudrillard, 1996a, p. 145.

69. Op. cit., Baudrillard, 1997, p. 74.

70. Op. cit., Baudrillard, 1994, p. 105.

71. Op. cit., Baudrillard, 1996a, p. 137.

72. Op. cit., Baudrillard, 1998, p. 59.

73. Ibid., p. 60.

74. Op. cit., Baudrillard, 1996a, p. 135.

75. See Michel Foucault, *The History of Sexuality, Volume 1: An Introduction*, London: Penguin, 1990.

76. Op. cit., Baudrillard, 1996a, p. 139.

77. Christopher Norris, *The Truth About Postmodernism*, Oxford: Blackwell, 1993, p. 63. See also Alex Callinicos, *Against Postmodernism: A Marxist critique*, Cambridge: Polity Press, 1989; Douglas Kellner, *Jean Baudrillard:*

from Marxism to postmodernism and beyond, Cambridge: Polity Press, 1989.

78. Zygmunt Bauman, 'The Sweet Scent of Decomposition', in Chris Rojek and Bryan S. Turner (eds.), *Forget Baudrillard*, London and New York: Routledge, 1993, p. 43.

79. Op. cit., Rojek and Turner (eds.), 1993, p. 110.

80. Op. cit., Baudrillard, 1996a, p. 95.

81. Op. cit., Baudrillard, 1998, p. 69.

82. Op. cit., Baudrillard, 1996a, p. 149.

83. Op. cit., Baudrillard, 1997, p. 98.

84. Op. cit., Baudrillard, 1998c, p. 8.

85. Ibid., p. 2.

Select Bibliography

Jean Baudrillard, *The Illusion of the End*, Cambridge: Polity Press, 1994.

Jean Baudrillard, *Simulacra and Simulation*, trans. Sheila Faria Glaser, Ann Arbor: University of Michigan Press, 1994a.

Jean Baudrillard, *The Gulf War did not take place*, trans. Paul Patton, University of Sydney: Power Institute, 1995.

Jean Baudrillard, *Cool Memories II: 1987–1990*, trans. Chris Turner, Cambridge: Polity Press, 1996.

Jean Baudrillard, *The Perfect Crime*, trans. Chris Turner, London and New York: Verso, 1996a.

Jean Baudrillard, *Fragments: Cool Memories III, 1991–95*, trans. Emily Agar, London and New York: Verso, 1997.

Jean Baudrillard, *Paroxysm: Interviews with Philippe Petit*, trans. Chris Turner, London and New York: Verso, 1998.

Jean Baudrillard, *In the Shadow of the Millennium (Or the Suspense of the Year 2000)*, trans. François Debrix, 1998b (Internet publication), http://www.ctheory.com/a61.html, 26 September 1998.

Jean Baudrillard, 'The End of the Millennium or The Countdown', *Theory, Culture and Society*, London: Sage, No. 1, February 1998c.

Key Ideas

The difficulty in reading and understanding Baudrillard and his version of the millennium is more stylistic than technical, as the scientific and philosophical terms he uses are clearly definable.

Pataphysics, for example, describes a science that makes up imaginary solutions, usually in opposition to the regular laws of physics or logic. Baudrillard uses this term to invert prevailing models of culture, technology and society.

In the same way, he borrows from recent theory in astrophysics in order to express the unseen, non-observable and radical forces that 'exist' at the limit of meaning and technology: **strange attractors** and **dark matter** are terms enlisted to connote the irresistible gravitational pull of the universe towards forces lying at its periphery. Baudrillard employs them in a cultural and social sense to suggest not simply the expansion of media and technological systems, but to suggest that they may be beholden to forces outside of rational, progressive, humanist processes.

The use of medical terminology such as **metastasis** (the transfer of disease from one distant location to another), **paroxysm** (a sudden and violent action) or **hysteresis** (the lagging of an effect behind a cause) are enlisted to describe respectively: the instantaneity of an event's dispersal by the media; the convulsive social events that occur at the end of the 20th century; and the continued proliferation of events even after their historical life has terminated.

The difficulty lies in Baudrillard's relatively terse, ironic and often aphoristic style of address. While this sometimes seems to obscure his arguments, a sustained reading of Baudrillard's key essays reveals a repeated set of 'moves' or strategies – most notably in the refusal to privilege positive, reconciled or resolved positions, as these would simply preserve the coercive accumulation of values to which our millennial culture aspires. Instead, Baudrillard advances neither a critique nor a negation of his millennial object, but *a more virulent version of it*, which exposes its form by adopting and exaggerating it.

With these key themes in mind we can, finally, summarise Baudrillard's millennium. The Year 2000 will not take place because: history itself is already a fiction, being only a culturally specific and constructed linear version of **events** linked by causes and effects; mass media **accelerates** events in all directions at once, thus escaping the space-time in which events make history (rather than just news); and because social and cultural processes of regression, atonement, **recycling**, management of **residues**, and laundering effectively place history in reverse. All of the 20th century's wars are happening again, backwards, and all freedoms are being withdrawn.

The millennium, however, is not the end, as the end is itself part of a linear version of history. Not even the end will take place, as the technoculture ensures that processes continue to unfold, but without meaning or sense. In this void, millennial, technological, digital and global culture has overstretched humanist, metaphysical and Enlightenment values. Catastrophic forms and **singularities** antagonistic to these universal values have erupted, often reversing the intended motives of those values. In addition to these reversals, the technoculture itself, in its viral, cancerous, metastatic form, has led to extreme and fatal proliferations in phenomena such as computer **viruses** or financial crashes beyond the controlling will of the rationalist, progressive enterprises that instigated them, and in exaggerated or ironic forms.

In conclusion, while we may be convinced by the hypothesis of the technological domination of the world by a fully integrated, obscene (over-exposed), saturated, simulated, **'objective' illusion** of 'reality', we should also be prepared to consider whether that dominated world (the object) is supplying us (the subject) with a more **radical illusion**: technology is a **ruse** that it uses in order to disappear quietly. It is, however, impossible to determine which hypothesis is true. Baudrillard's millennium behaves, I would argue, like a **quantum** one: either condition is simultaneously and possibly true. Just as the observation and experiment by the scientist affects from the outset the direction of rotation of an observed atom, so too does our view of the millennium generate and thus prove one or other hypothesis – **disappearance** or **simulation** – according, it might be suggested, to our whim.

Acknowledgements

My thanks go to Jean Baudrillard, Duncan Heath, Cristina Mateo, Toby Clark, Fran Lloyd, Valerie Merlo and John Dutton.

Other titles available in the Postmodern Encounters series from Icon/Totem

Derrida and the End of History
Stuart Sim
ISBN 1 84046 094 6
UK £2.99   USA $7.95

What does it mean to proclaim 'the end of history', as several thinkers have done in recent years? Francis Fukuyama, the American political theorist, created a considerable stir in *The End of History and the Last Man* (1992) by claiming that the fall of communism and the triumph of free market liberalism brought an 'end of history' as we know it. Prominent among his critics has been the French philosopher Jacques Derrida, whose *Specters of Marx* (1993) deconstructed the concept of 'the end of history' as an ideological confidence trick, in an effort to salvage the unfinished and ongoing project of democracy.

Derrida and the End of History places Derrida's claim within the context of a wider tradition of 'endist' thought. Derrida's critique of endism is highlighted as one of his most valuable contributions to the postmodern cultural debate – as well as being the most accessible entry to *deconstruction*, the controversial philosophical movement founded by him.

Foucault and Queer Theory
Tamsin Spargo
ISBN 1 84046 092 X
UK £2.99   USA $7.95

Michel Foucault is the most gossiped-about celebrity
of French poststructuralist theory. The homophobic
insult 'queer' is now proudly reclaimed by some who
once called themselves lesbian or gay. What is the
connection between the two? This is a postmodern
encounter between Foucault's theories of sexuality,
power and discourse and the current key exponents
of queer thinking who have adopted, revised and
criticised Foucault. Our understanding of gender,
identity, sexuality and cultural politics will be radically
altered in this meeting of transgressive figures.

Nietzsche and Postmodernism
Dave Robinson
ISBN 1 84046 093 8
UK £2.99   USA $7.95

Friedrich Nietzsche (1844–1900) has exerted a huge
influence on 20th century philosophy and literature. He
questioned what it means for us to live in our modern
world, and expressed grave reservations about the
reliability of human knowledge. His radical scepticism
disturbs our deepest-held beliefs, and casts a 'long
shadow' on the complex cultural and philosophical
phenomenon we now call 'postmodernism'. *Nietzsche
and Postmodernism* explains the key ideas of this 'Anti-
Christ' philosopher and concludes by asking if Nietzsche
can justifiably be called the first great postmodernist.

Einstein and the Total Eclipse
Peter Coles
ISBN 1 84046 089 X
UK £2.99   USA $7.95

In ancient times, the duration of a total solar eclipse was a time of fear and wonder. The scientific revolution that began with Copernicus relegated these eclipses to the category of 'understood' phenomena. Astronomers still relish their occurrence, not because of the event itself, but because of the opportunity it provides to carry out observations that would otherwise be impossible by day.

This book is about a famous example of this opportunism: the two expeditions to observe the bending of starlight by the Sun – predicted by Einstein's general theory of relativity – from Sobral in northern Brazil and the island of Principe in the Gulf of Guinea during the eclipse of 29 May 1919.

As well as providing a simple way of understanding the key ideas of Einstein's theory, this story offers fascinating insights into the sociological conflicts between 'Big Science' and popular culture that are as real today as they were 80 years ago.